YOUR COMPANION THROUGH **GRIEF**

GRETA SMITH

OUT OF THE DEPTHS

Nashville

OUT OF THE DEPTHS:
YOUR COMPANION THROUGH GRIEF

Copyright © 2018 by Abingdon Press

This book is printed on acid-free paper.

978-1-5018-7130-6

18 19 20 21 22 23 24 25 26 27—10 9 8 7 6 5 4 3 2 1

MANUFACTURED IN THE UNITED STATES OF AMERICA

CONTENTS

INTRODUCTION

There's a season for everything
and a time for every matter under the heavens:
a time for giving birth and a time for dying,
a time for planting and a time for uprooting what was planted,
a time for killing and a time for healing,
a time for tearing down and a time for building up,
a time for crying and a time for laughing,
a time for mourning and a time for dancing,
a time for throwing stones and a time for gathering stones,
a time for embracing and a time for avoiding embraces,
a time for searching and a time for losing,
a time for keeping and a time for throwing away,
a time for tearing and a time for repairing,
a time for keeping silent and a time for speaking,
a time for loving and a time for hating,
a time for war and a time for peace.

—Ecclesiastes 3:1-8

My times are in your hands; deliver me from the hands of my
enemies, from those who pursue me.

—Psalm 31:15 (NIV)

I have a very specific early memory about the certainty and finality of death. I was about four years old. My favorite television show at the time, Isis, chronicled the adventures of a female superhero. I loved Isis, and she was a consistent Saturday morning presence in our home, as well as being my imaginary companion much of the time. Isis is a teacher who discovers an amulet which enables her to turn into an Egyptian goddess and to have superpowers such as superhuman strength, speed, and the ability to fly.

I do not remember all of the details about this particular episode, but I remember that a young boy was saved from drowning. He had a dog named Lucky. I remember that Lucky played some role in the boy's rescue, and sadly, died as a result. I remember the boy crying over his precious friend. I remember his sadness and his anger. But here is the part I remember most vividly: Isis explained the cycle of life and death to the boy with the words, "Everything that lives must one day die." As she spoke, the television screen showed a flower, a single shoot, sprouting, blossoming, opening, and then withering and dying. That image became ingrained in my consciousness. My four-year-old world was shaken.

Before that day, I had a limited understanding of death, namely that it was something that happened when a person or animal was sick or had a terrible accident. I knew on some level that it was irreversible. But I had never considered that *my* dog, or cat, let alone my *mom* or *dad* might one day die.

I ran into the laundry room where my mother was moving clothes from the washer to the dryer. "Mom!" I exclaimed, "Isis just said that everything dies; that flowers die; and animals die and people, too. Is that true?"

My mom was taken aback. In her eyes I saw her make a split-second decision. She would not lie to me.

"Yes, honey, it is." She went on to reassure me, as best she could, that she and my dad were not going to die for a long, long time. But the world changed for me that day. Although at that tender age I had not yet experienced a significant loss, just the knowledge of its possibility was enough to shatter my innocence.

Sooner or later, we must all confront the truth of those words— everything that lives must one day die. And not only that, but everything that starts must one day end. We lose those we love through literal death. But we also lose relationships, roles, aspects of personality which have come to represent something significant, sometimes integral, even, to our sense of ourselves. Life is fraught with loss. Most of us maintain some awareness of this truth, even though it is unconscious most of the time, even though we must repress or deny it in our day-to-day moving and going about in the world, simply in order to function. And then the day comes—and for most of us it comes not once but repeatedly—when death, loss, or tragedy sweeps in and destroys our world in a way that cannot be ignored. We are left floundering, trying to find some solid ground on which to stand, attempting to pick up the shattered pieces of our lives and put them back together in some way that makes it possible to live again.

The great Wisdom literature of the Bible shows that God's people have always struggled with loss and have wrestled specifically with how to reconcile the goodness of God with the suffering of the world. There are no easy answers, but we have learned much about the process of grief and continue to understand the importance of ancient faith practices and the wisdom of grieving through ritual and in community. Finding hope and meaning in suffering is a quest shared by God's people, even though each of us experiences loss differently and even when it feels as though we walk alone.

This little book is intended to be a companion in grief. It is organized into two parts. The first is educational. In it, we will look at five basic things to know about the grief process. It is my sincere hope that this knowledge will provide a useful framework within which to understand your personal experience of grief. The second part of the book is devotional, and consists of thirty daily scripture readings, devotions and prayers. It is my sincere prayer that these readings will bring hope and comfort, provide a daily grounding faith ritual, and lend a sense of connectedness, both to God and to a community of grieving hearts, as you move through the days and weeks to come. You do not have to read the first part of this book before beginning the devotions. Feel free to start them at any time.

A natural part of being human is the desire to understand and to order our experience. Common questions about grief include:

- What can I expect?

- How long will I feel this way?

- Is what I am feeling or experiencing normal?

- What can I do about it?

Having a general framework for grief and knowing what the common experience is and what you might expect (loosely) can itself be comforting. And while there are no quick fixes for the pain of loss, there are things that can help us cope and endure the pain as we heal. Most of the time, grief is a normal process that follows its own natural and healthy course. However, it is also important to be able to recognize when this is not the case, and when to seek additional help. Toward these ends, we will look at five things to know about grief:

1. **Grief is all-encompassing.** Grief affects all aspects of our human experience. It is physical, emotional, mental, spiritual, and social, and you may experience "symptoms" of grief in all of these areas.

2. **Grief is individualized.** While stage, task, and other theories of grief can help us understand common experiences during grief, people rarely fit into a mold, and we do not grieve in stages, phases, or by accomplishing specific tasks.

3. **Grief takes time.** Grief takes its own time, and often, grief takes a lifetime. When it comes to our greatest, life-changing losses, it is not accurate or helpful to talk about grief as a finite process. Rather, how we grieve, and how grief affects us, changes over the course of time and within context.

4. **Grief cannot be controlled.** We cannot control the grief process, or our own healing, but we can employ helpful means of coping. There are things we can do to help ourselves manage some of the physical, emotional, mental, spiritual, and social symptoms of grief.

5. **Grief can be complicated.** Complicated grief does not necessarily follow a normal healing process, but help is available.

The contents of this book draw from my experience as a practicing mental health professional, as a pastor-in-training, and as someone who has grieved deeply. The same year that I received my license to practice psychology, I lost my firstborn daughter unexpectedly in a tragic end to an uncomplicated pregnancy. I had carried her for eight months, but my daughter lived only two days. I am proof positive that the length of a relationship does not directly correlate with the depth of grief. Emma Grace's death remains the greatest heartbreak of my life.

If this little book has found its way into your hands, please know that I am deeply sorry. You and I share the experience of a loss that is life-altering and a grief that is self-compromising. Our greatest losses change us in a way that is irreparable. However, even though our deepest losses cannot be repaired, they can be redeemed. This is the good news of Christ for the people of God. It is our greatest hope—that when all is lost, even literally, God's redemptive power is already at work. I pray that you will see evidence of this power at work in your life—and in your loss—even as we continue to grieve together.

*God, in my broken-heartedness, remind me that all my times
are in your hands. In the weeping and laughing, mourning and
dancing—in every season—you are with me, as you have been with
the ancestors of my faith and remain with all of humanity in our
shared experiences of loss, suffering, and grief. May I cling to your
goodness, grace, and mercy. Speak gently to my spirit, that I may
find hope in the healing that is to come. Amen.*

Blessings and peace,
Greta Smith

Chapter One

GRIEF IS ALL-ENCOMPASSING

Grief affects all aspects of our human experience. Sadness is, of course, the hallmark symptom of grief. It is so pervasive and encompassing that much of the time I think we tend to equate grief with sadness. Acknowledging and expressing sadness are essential functions of the griever, but equating grief with sadness can be problematic on many accounts. Perhaps the most important one is this: when we do not look or feel sad, others may think that we are no longer grieving. In fact, we sometimes deceive ourselves into the sense that we are not—or should not be—grieving, because our sadness is no longer observable.

Researchers who have dedicated their professional lives to the study of grief can tell us that loss not only triggers common psychological responses, but also physical and relational ones. Psychologically, we easily think of grief as emotional, but it can have cognitive, perceptual, and spiritual implications as well. Even limiting our consideration to the emotional aspects of grief, sadness is what we think of most, but anxiety, panic, anger, hostility, irritability, impatience, guilt, regret, frustration, loneliness, yearning, helplessness, apathy, and relief are other common emotions experienced.

Grief can alter our cognitive functioning as well. Perhaps you have seen distractibility, disorganization, impaired decision making, diminished concentration, and pessimism or lack of interest, motivation, or initiative in others who have experienced a monumental loss. In all likelihood, it was not surprising to you to witness those struggles. However, you may have been unprepared for them yourself. Many times, I have heard grieving people describe episodes of "not thinking straight" and then, with a puzzled look, comment, "I don't know what's the matter with me." Of course, the matter was grief.

Perhaps most unsettling are the perceptual disturbances that can accompany grief. The sense that things are not real, that one is not oneself or is absent from one's body, or a sense of dread, the continuous feeling that something bad is about to happen, can be frightening. So can auditory or visual extrasensory experiences. But hearing or seeing the one you have lost, or feeling a sense of his or her presence, can be comforting as well. Depending on a person's background and culture, all of these experiences may fall within the range of a normal grief response.

Life-changing loss can also bring about a spiritual crisis. Hopelessness, despair, a sense of meaninglessness, spiritual confusion, and feelings of spiritual alienation are common. But so are increased spirituality and a renewed search for meaning. Faith can help us cope with loss, or it can be deeply shaken, and these are not mutually exclusive experiences, either. Either or both are normal.

As you can see, uncomplicated grief can take many forms, and even vastly contrasting responses can still be considered typical. This becomes especially important to keep in mind when you are evaluating the grief of others who shared the same, or a similar, relationship with the one you have lost.

Sleep and appetite disturbance may be the physical symptoms most readily associated with grief, but a myriad of other physical responses can be observed. Sleep disturbance can include sleeping too much, sleeping too little, having trouble falling asleep, or waking frequently. Appetite disturbance could mean loss of appetite with weight loss or increased eating with weight gain. Deep sighing, fatigue, low energy, feeling easily exhausted, and trouble remembering or concentrating fall loosely within the category of symptoms professionals identify under the label "psychomotor retardation." Trembling, shaking, twitching, restlessness, searching, pacing, and feeling as if your mind won't be still or turn off fall loosely within the category we label as "psychomotor agitation." Headaches, heart palpitations, shortness of breath, dizziness, nausea, trouble swallowing, numbness and tingling, all of these are commonly reported by people experiencing grief! In fact, almost any physical ailment can be found in the list of physical responses, including vague, diffuse physical complaints which come in waves and can last minutes to hours. Grieving parents, in particular (myself included), have described muscle pain, aches, and soreness. In other words, sometimes, our arms literally ache for the ones we love. It is always a good idea to talk to your doctor about any new physical symptoms you are experiencing, but if you have had a thorough physical exam and received a clean bill of health from your provider, your unusual aches and pains may be a sign of grief.

For many of us, the social or relational experience of grief is one of the most difficult aspects of the grieving process, and surprisingly so. We can be caught off guard by the way grief alters our relationships with others. There are at least two reasons for this that I can identify. One is that when we are grieving we tend to pull away from others. The second is that when we are grieving others tend to pull away from us.

Why do we pull away from others while we grieve? A griever's tendency toward social withdrawal is made worse by the loss of interest, motivation, and energy that relationships require. So much of our energy during grief is focused inwardly that there are not a lot of reserves for the maintenance of existing relationships, let alone the development of new ones. In addition, there is an alienating quality to the griever's experience of the world. It is hard to relate to the day-to-day concerns of most of the population when it feels as though the ground has fallen out from under your feet. Making casual conversation can be insufferable.

Second, people sometimes pull away, even unconsciously, from those who grieve. Afraid of saying or doing the wrong thing, they do or say nothing at all. Even the carefulness of another person's words and actions can be experienced as alienating. When people treat us differently, even if it is because of their sensitivity to our feelings, they are still treating us differently. Sometimes we welcome this as compassionate, but at other times it highlights the isolation we feel, when what we need and long for most is a sense of connectedness. And no discussion of grief and relationships would be complete without acknowledgement of those who cavalierly do and/or say the wrong thing without any sensitivity at all. Their words and actions open and deepen our wounds and are not easily forgotten. Because this is retraumatizing, those of us who have suffered exponential loss can often, even years later, quote verbatim the worst things people said to us when we were raw with grief.

Relationships are changed and sometimes lost, when we are grieving. Mental health folks refer to these as "secondary losses." Secondary losses can include not only the shifting or ending of significant relationships, but also the loss of role and identity, places, patterns, and routines that have been a significant part of our lives, hopes and dreams about the future, or any of the cluster of losses that accompany the death of a loved one. For example, if you have recently lost an aging parent, you might also have lost the relationship with a caregiver who had become a significant part of your life and with whom you had bonded. You might be losing the home you grew up in, and you might feel that you have lost your role and identity as a son or daughter. All of these are second-ary losses for which you also grieve.

Two things are worth emphasizing in our consideration of social and relational responses to grief. Social support is a vital part of coping and healing during grief. While you may not have the energy or inclina-tion to reach out or nurture a lot of relationships, be careful not to ne-glect the ones that are most important. It is okay to withdraw some and for a while. Some relationships may be changed in a way that is irrepa-rable and that is okay, too. Exponential losses or major life transitions have a way of clarifying for us the things and people that really matter most. Shutting yourself off completely, however, is neither a short-term solution nor an effective means of defending yourself against future grief or pain.

In choosing which relationships to invest the most time and energy in right now, keep in mind a couple of things. As you have seen from this discussion, grief can take many forms. There is an almost endless range of normal grief responses. So, if your brother or sister does not seem to be grieving for your mother or father as you are, this does not mean that he or she is not grieving at all. Just because you cannot under-stand your spouse's response to your son or daughter's death, it is not fair to assume he or she feels less pain than you do. Give the people closest to you, who are likely grieving too, room to grieve in their own time and in their own way. Focus on the love you share for the one you have lost and not on the differences in the ways you have responded to their death.

Additionally, when you can, and especially when a friendship has been very significant to you, give people the benefit of the doubt. Be forgiving of their blunders. Remember, the chances are good that you have unintentionally offended someone else in their grief. Perhaps you realized after the fact that you said something insensitive, and you were horrified. Hardly anyone wants to add to another person's pain, espe-cially to the pain of those we dearly love. Try to see beyond the hurtful words or actions to the intention. Often our friends are trying to do or say the things they think will be the least hurtful, but they make the wrong choice. Think of the motive, not the outcome, of their behavior. Consider talking with them about what would be helpful to you in similar situations in the future.

Months after my daughter died, a friend from college called to tell me that she had given birth to a daughter. I did not even know she had been pregnant. I was hurt, because one of our mutual friends—my *best* friend, who was calling me regularly—knew of the pregnancy but had not told me. She thought she was protecting me, but I felt caught off guard and excluded. We had a difficult conversation about this. In fact, we had several difficult conversations. Our relationship was strained by my grief for a long time. Thankfully, though, we did not give up on each other. As a result, our friendship is stronger than it was before and has a depth that few ever achieve. I consider this to be a gift from my daughter, beauty from the ashes of my grief.

Chapter Two

GRIEF IS INDIVIDUALIZED

In 1969, when Elisabeth Kübler-Ross published her well known but generally misunderstood book *On Death and Dying,* it was revolutionary.[1] Kübler-Ross had the boldness and the open-mindedness to bring dying into the public consciousness. At the time, death and grief had become a solitary experience, even though throughout much of history and across many cultures, people had grieved collectively. Relegated to the individual, death became closed off from the larger community. People with terminal illness regularly died alone, in hospitals. Moreover, they were not often given accurate information about their medical conditions or terminal status. Doctors did not know how to talk to patients about dying.

Into this atmosphere entered Kübler-Ross, who had the audacity and insight to talk to dying people about their impending deaths. She noticed common themes in the narratives of these dying patients, and from her interviews with them she formulated a stage theory for the psychological process of death and dying. Because she also observed that the family members of dying patients demonstrated some of the same themes, she postulated that they progress through the stages too.

Kübler-Ross's stages—denial, anger, bargaining, depression, and acceptance—eventually became taken up by the popular culture as "the five stages of grief," in spite of the fact that she developed them from her observations of dying and not grieving people and in spite of the subsequent lack of empirical support.

The positive outcome of Kübler-Ross's research was the way in which it has changed the experience of death and dying. Her research paved the way for the hospice movement, and for improved education for doctors around care of the dying. The inadvertent negative outcome is perhaps the limiting way her stage theory has led us to talk about grief and to understand it for ourselves and for one another. We try to fit our experience of grief into the five stages. I have even heard people ask a grieving person, "Which stage are you in?"

Maybe it was the illusion of control suggested by the stage theory of grief that made it so appealing to the masses. And there is a truth to the theory in that these psychological processes Kübler-Ross identified are often seen in both dying and in grieving. But they are not the experience of everyone, and people do not progress through them in any linear fashion.

Kübler-Ross had been influenced in the development of her theory by the work of a British psychiatrist named John Bowlby and his colleague Collin Murray Parkes. Bowlby became particularly interested in the ways we connect with others through observing and working with children who had been separated from their parents. Parkes and Bowlby proposed that there are four overlapping phases or stages of grief: numbness and shock, searching and yearning, disorganization and despair, and reorganization and recovery.[2]

Other researchers have suggested that grieving successfully involves accomplishing a series of tasks, such as accepting the reality of the loss, experiencing the pain of grief, adjusting to the new environment without the deceased, and finding an enduring connection with the deceased while embarking on a new life.[3] Grief expert and researcher Therese Rando offers a similar task theory, involving the "Six R" processes: recognition of the loss, reaction to the separation of it, remembering and re-experiencing the relationship, relinquishing old attachments and assumptions about the world, and readjusting to move into a new world, adaptively.[4]

Recent theorists have also proposed that grief is interactional, and involves many factors, including the characteristics of the individual and the relationship, which determine its course. They have found that grief varies across individuals and within the same individual, from moment to moment.[5] In addition, current researchers suggest that most people get better on their own, and there are, in reality, no stages or tasks to work through and no right or wrong way to grieve.[6] However, some have suggested that grief does tend to come in "waves," which can be described as either loss-oriented (the pangs of grief we identified before) or restoration-oriented (including positive emotions, such as laughter and joy, which give a respite from the loss).[7]

My favorite academic writers and grief theorists are the ones who study grief from the perspective of narrative. These writers describe grief in terms of a person's life narrative.[8] Their description of the process of grief resonates with mine. One truth the world over is that we are a storied people. From the beginning of recorded history, humans have attempted to make sense of the world, collectively, and individually, by creating stories. Our brains seemed to be wired for it. We describe the events of our individual and communal lives in storied form. Our identity is found, or made, in stories.

In any story, there are critical turning points, places in which the characters face adversity, or conflict. The tone, action, and plot of the story change. Generally, we can look back at our lives and identify our own critical turning points, the times and places in which everything changed for us. Often these are associated with a loss of some kind.

When we encounter a crisis, our understanding of ourselves and the world is challenged. The things we take for granted are called into question. Our experience of the world is changed, and it may no longer seem like the relatively safe or predictable place it was before. Perhaps, for example, we cannot imagine a world without the one we have lost and are unsure how we can possibly live in such a world.

Narrative theorists suggest that when faced with such a dilemma, we either have to somehow *assimilate* the crisis or loss into our existing understanding of how the world operates or change that understanding in order to *accommodate* the loss. Or, for most of us, this process of coping with loss involves both assimilation and accommodation.[9] For people of faith, this process often involves reexamining our understanding of God and beliefs about how God is in relation to God's people.

My daughter's death precipitated a crisis of faith. If you had asked me before I lost Emma, I would have acknowledged that experiencing the death of a child is not a punishment for wicked behavior and that living a righteous life does not protect a person against such loss, and yet there was a sense in which I lived with just such an expectation. Much like my four-year-old world was shattered with the knowledge that death could touch my family as I described at the beginning of this book, my twenty-nine-year-old world was shattered by the experience of losing my baby. I knew that I lived in a world in which God allowed babies to die. Somehow, though, that world was different from the one in which God allowed my baby to die. Part of grief became, for me, realizing the unconscious expectations I had in my relationship with God and allowing them to be changed.

For this reason and others, I would describe my own grief as a process of integration. Initially, Emma's death was so monumental that it overshadowed every part of my life. In fact, it shattered my very identity. Everything I knew or thought I knew, everything I experienced had to be re-evaluated in light of her death. My grief was a huge amorphous central and defining entity. Over time, though, it has become integrated into my experience of myself, the world, and myself in the world. It no longer overshadows everything about my life or being. It never leaves me; it is a part of me. But it is not all of me. It is a part of my story but not the entirety of it.

For narrative theorists, an important part of grieving well is finding meaning in and through, loss. We will explore more in the next section, but if you are struggling with the need to find meaning, you are not alone. It is a central part of grief for many people.

The problem with all of these theories, though, is that they are limited in their application to real human beings. While interesting, they are not necessarily helpful. They can be helpful only inasmuch as they are helpful to you, in your particular grief. And if you decide to learn about any of them, this is how you should evaluate their merit in your circumstance. It is unlikely that any of them will completely capture or describe the course of your grief. People (and especially human relationships) do not fit neatly into prescribed theories or molds.

No one else has ever had the particular relationship you are grieving. No one experienced your beloved in exactly the same way that you did. Your relationship was exactly like no other. Your loss was exactly like no other, and your grief will be exactly like no other. And this knowledge will at times be oddly comforting, and at times extremely isolating. Because with it comes the understanding that while we grieve best in community and we were made to grieve together, there is also a way in which you must grieve alone. No one can enter completely into your grief.

In your grief, you may, as I said, find it helpful to learn about theories of grief. If they speak to your experience and help you find a language for your loss or a frame for your experience, then accept what they have to offer you. However, be wary of using them to create expectations of yourself and your grief.

Chapter Three

GRIEF TAKES TIME

As I mentioned in the previous chapter, grief is a highly individualized process. In that section we addressed what makes it highly individualized. In this section, we will look at what it means that grief is a process.

It is best to think of grief as a progression, and not a state or a quality. As C. S. Lewis wrote of his own grief, "I thought I could describe a state, make a map of sorrow. Sorrow, however, turns out not to be a state but a process. It needs not a map but a history."[1] What Lewis is referring to is the experience that grief takes on a life of its own. It is not so much a state that you move in or out of as it is a relational experience in its own right. Grief shifts and changes over time and never really goes away. It becomes not so much the territory in which you reside as *you* become the territory in which *it* resides. Grief has its own story and timeline. Often, grief takes a lifetime.

Take for example the loss of the most primary relationship we have. For most of us, this would be the maternal relationship, but it could be anyone you considered to be your primary caregiver from birth. It is inconceivable to think that there ever would come a time in which that relationship stopped being significant to us. This, our first experience with care, trust, love, and nurture, lives in us and affects us throughout our lives. Whether we become estranged from our primary caregivers or separated from them by death, it is nearly impossible to think there will come a time when we have completed our grief over that loss. What would "completed" even mean? What would that look like? By completion of grief we certainly would not mean that we have forgotten the relationship. Do we expect to come to a place where we never feel sad or a place in which sadness no longer dominates our recollection? Do we expect never to revisit painful or conflicted feelings? In other words, how would we know that we have successfully "finished" grieving?

Most of the time, when we talk about a timeline for grief, I think we mean to suggest that there naturally comes a time when our grief does not dominate our experience of the world. It is less the air we breathe than the ground we walk on. Remember those ambiguous black and white drawings that shift depending whether you are looking at the black or white as figural? The picture itself does not change, but your perception of it does. And so it is with grief. The loss does not go away, but our experience of grief changes.

There is a wide range to what can be considered normal in this respect. Many people report that acute grief climaxes at about six months and that the first year following a significant loss is hardest, but this is not true for everyone. Acute grief can last two years or more, particularly if you are grieving the loss of a spouse or a child or if the death was shocking or especially traumatic. For many people, the first year is especially hard, as it is a year of firsts: first birthdays, first holidays, and first anniversaries of significant events, including the day of death. But many people are deceived into thinking that making it through the first year following a loss is somehow magical and have the mistaken impression that all will become easier following that first anniversary. This is rarely the case. And holiday and anniversary grief can continue indefinitely.

One of the reasons that grief is not experienced as a finite process has to do with the cumulative nature of grief and with the ways in which grief changes according to our context. For example, consider an aging person who has experienced the loss of both parents and a number of close friends. Now she experiences the death of a spouse. Of course, she will grieve for her spouse specifically and acutely. But once the most intense and figural aspects of that particular grief have passed, even if it has taken years, it would not be at all surprising if she continues to struggle with an overall sense of loss and with how to adapt to a world absent of many of the most important people in her life.

Now imagine that she has a health crisis. She loses functioning and mobility, and her day-to-day life changes again rapidly. She may not only more intensely miss her husband or find herself revisiting memories of his deteriorating health and her experience as his caregiver, but she will likely grieve over her limitations, the things she can no longer enjoy, and her loss of independence. All of this is within the context of a world that continues to change rapidly for her and which has been fraught with loss.

Following the death of our daughter, my husband and I experienced infertility. In the ensuing years of treatment and the roller coaster of disappointment and continuing loss, it was often difficult for me to tease apart the sorrow I felt over Emma, the grief of miscarriage, and the fear of the loss of motherhood. In fact, paradoxically, they were both inseparable *and* independent. I grieved each, and I grieved them together.

Now consider the example of a boy who loses his father as a child. His childhood grief will not look the same as his adult grief. And we would not expect him to "finish" grieving for his father within two years after the death. He is likely to experience grief differently as he matures. Think of when he learns to drive, goes on his first date, gets married, or becomes a father himself. All of these life events create a new context within which he might grieve differently. He will remember his father and miss him differently. He will long for the different roles in which he experienced his dad, such as teacher, mentor, or advice-giver and roles which he never got the chance to witness, like grandfather.

My grief for my daughter has waxed and waned over 17 years now. Babies who were born at the same time as she was are now getting ready to go to college. I cannot help but revisit "what if," a question I once thought had buried itself forever. I also find that as my children become more independent and knowing that I am past childbearing age, I cannot help but revisit my grief over infertility. Though I love watching my children grow, I sometimes miss the unsurpassed joy of having a baby in my arms.

Grief does not dominate my daily living, but it is present in my consciousness. At times it seems dormant, and at times it awakens, but as I said, I live with it as its own entity. I do not expect that it will ever go away completely. Most likely, neither will your own grief ever go away completely.

I do not share these examples to depress or demoralize you. As you will see in the next section, people are surprisingly resilient. Just as grief persists, so does recovery and coping. But I want you to consider that grief is complex. We do not grieve neatly and according to a particular time frame. Living as a human being is messy. We never know what is coming around the corner. Grief can be messy, too.

One of the best answers I have heard to the question, "How long does grief take?" is "It takes as long as it takes." Know that you can naturally expect grief to become less dominant in the landscape of your life. Sometimes the most painful part of grief does not come until months after the loss, and I do not want you to be surprised by that. But sometime during or after the first year, you will likely find that grieving is not your primary activity. And if for you it takes longer than a year, or even two, know that is most likely okay, too.

Chapter Four

GRIEF CANNOT BE CONTROLLED

G rief is a paradox and an enigma. We cannot control the process of grief or our own healing, but we can employ helpful means of coping. There is a sense in which we actively grieve, and a sense in which grief is something that happens to us, or even in spite of us. I have often said that dealing with grief is kind of like looking at the sun. You can never really look directly at it, and even after looking in its direction, sometimes you have to look completely away. But it continues shining whether you are looking at it or not.

We do not necessarily decide when to look in the direction of grief and when to look away. Our minds take care of this unconsciously, with the waves of grief discussed before. Loss-oriented waves are sort of like looking in the direction of the sun, and restoration-oriented waves are sort of like looking away. Still, even though these emotions are not chosen consciously, many people struggle the first time they realize they have laughed or experienced joy, in the wake of grief. They feel a pang of guilt, as if they have done something wrong or somehow betrayed their sadness over the absence of their beloved.

Both the experience of joy and the guilt over it are common experiences during grief. Awareness of laughter or joy (a restoration-oriented wave) leading to guilt leading to sadness (another loss-oriented wave) are a frequent pattern at first. Over time, you are likely to find that you can laugh or feel joy without the same guilt and that your laughter or joy may even evoke positive memories of your loved one. Remember that we are uniquely capable of having mixed feelings, and it is possible to feel both happy and sad at the same time. In fact, it is so common, we have a name for it: bittersweet.

So, in many ways, grief is a natural process that you cannot control. You cannot necessarily speed it up, for example (although some research has suggested that grief counseling can help along the process of normal grief).[1] However, there are things you can do to help yourself heal, and ways in which you can actively cope.

To begin with, healing from grief (or from any psychological trauma) is much like healing from a physical illness in that good health behaviors are good health behaviors and support all manner of health and healing. In other words, the more you are able to get an adequate amount of rest, eat well, limit your intake of alcohol and caffeine, exercise, surround yourself with people you love and who love you, and engage in the things that bring you meaning and joy, the more you are supporting your health, healing, and general wellness. Foremost, then, take care of yourself much like you would take care of someone else to help them heal from an injury or to promote their wellbeing.

Additionally, remember that for thousands of years, people have grieved in community, and this was probably not by accident. As I write this, I am sitting downstairs in a room in my home church. There is a funeral going on in the sanctuary above me. It is the funeral of someone I did not know, but I can hear the organ playing a hymn I recognize, and I hear muffled voices raised in a song of praise. After the service is over, the family will likely gather for a meal prepared by friends.

As people of faith, we give worship and give thanks for the life of God's children after their death. A funeral is a worship service, but it is also a way for a community to surround the family of those who have died with love and support. It is one of the few ways in which we continue to do so in our culture, but throughout the ages and in many cultures around the world people have grieved together, in community. In many cultures the families of the deceased have symbolized their grief in various ways for months or even a full year, and the people surrounding them were therefore reminded to treat them with care.

Culture has always been a primary determinant of the ways in which people grieve. A culture teaches its inhabitants what is normative and provides the rituals that mark the major life transitions, including death and loss. When I visit the cemetery, I see flowers everywhere, on almost every grave. Because I have grown up in a culture in which decorating graves with flowers is common, I am not surprised by this sight. Every now and then, however, I see a plate of fruit. Placing fruit on graves is not customary where I am from, so I always find it unexpected. However, I am reminded that those from other cultures might find the sight of flowers odd. Cultural practices will largely influence the expression of grief in any society.

Currently, we live in one of the most death denying and avoidant cultures in the world, and perhaps in history. We expect people to go back to their "normal" lives, often immediately after the funeral of a loved one, or after their three-day bereavement leave is over and they have returned to work. It is not lost on me that I am here writing about grief within earshot of a funeral. Death and grief are a part of life, and especially part of the life of the church. It concerns me, though, that we have largely forgotten how to grieve together, in community.

You and I may not be able to force our culture to grieve collectively the way that many other cultures did and do, but we can recognize that the history of grief was perhaps born of an understanding of human need that we have forgotten. We can use this knowledge to help ourselves in our grief. For example, many people find comfort in rituals of remembrance. We may not routinely cover our heads or wear black armbands to symbolize our grief to others, but you can still choose your own personally meaningful ritual. A friend of mine wore an angel pin in memory of her son daily following his death. Others might wear lockets or light candles. There was a time in which I prayed Psalm 40 daily. I also kept a daily journal. If you are a writer or find solace in expressing your thoughts and feelings, you may want to do the same. Research has shown health benefits of journaling our emotional experience.[2] My journal became a saving grace for me.

If you are more physically expressive than emotionally expressive, your ritual may involve daily exercise, or you may want to give yourself a new challenge or take up a new sport. While I journaled my grief, my husband trained for his first marathon. There can also be something healing about focusing on the thing you can control when much of your life and emotions seem out of your control, as in grief.

Just as grief is highly individualized, coping with grief can be highly individualized, too. Again, give others around you the room they need to grieve and permission to grieve in their own way. And remember that there is no right or wrong way to grieve. If someone you love does not seem to be grieving as you think they should, or wish they would and you are concerned that they are delaying their grief response in a way that will come back to haunt them, become informed. Researchers now believe that there is no such thing as delayed grief.[3] So do not try to force someone else to grieve in the way you want them to. Consider that your unacceptance of the way in which they are grieving may indicate something you need to work through rather than something they need to work on.

Because we have lost much of the communal expression of grief, connectedness may be something we have to consciously search for in our grief. Reading this book is an example of one way in which to connect. You may find comfort and connectedness in other books or memoirs as well. Many people find it helpful to connect directly with other people who are grieving, especially those who are grieving a similar loss. There are grief support groups for general grief, but also for widows and widowers, grieving parents, families who have lost a loved one to suicide, and others. Your local funeral homes, churches, hospitals, or hospice centers likely maintain lists of support groups for grief in your area. In this digital age, you may also find helpful resources and groups online.

Because the narrative approach to grief has been most useful for me in my work with grieving people, I want to suggest to you three things that you may find helpful as you try to cope and support your own healing. In the 1970s and 80s an American-Israeli medical sociologist by the name of Aaron Antonovsky published his work on a theory of health, a field he called *salutogenesis*, or the origins of health. He was interested in how people cope and even thrive following major stresses or traumatic events. Much of his work was done with Holocaust survivors who appeared to be emotionally healthy, a fact that he found astounding. From his interviews with them, he developed a theory of health, or positive coping with stress that he called "sense of coherence."[4]

Antonovsky suggested that there are three important aspects to coping with a traumatic experience, in our case a loss, that are related to maintaining a sense of coherence. They are comprehensibility, manageability, and meaningfulness. Comprehensibility refers to the extent to which a person has an understanding of the reasons a trauma or loss occurred and can therefore maintain a sense of the world as generally predictable. An example would be knowing the cause of death of your beloved. Though such knowledge does not help make the death more acceptable, it is likely to help make it more understandable. Manageability describes the extent to which a person believes he or she has the skills, ability, resources or support to deal with a trauma or loss. For example, this might refer to the sense that even though your heart is broken and life will never be the same, you believe it is possible to go on living, to cope, and to recover. Meaningfulness refers to the belief that life remains worthwhile and that you can experience joy and purpose again. It may also include the desire to see meaning come from the trauma or loss itself.

As your grief becomes part of your story, I encourage you to think about these things—comprehensibility, manageability, and meaningfulness—especially in light of your faith. Is the death of the one you have lost comprehensible to you? Do you understand what happened? If not, is there some way you can get answers or someone who can help you understand what happened? Sometimes comprehensibility can come from an awareness or acceptance that God has ordered the universe in a certain way, with laws of physics, for example, that do not change. These laws help us to live predictably most of the time, even if we wish they would bend sometimes. Gravity was a factor in the circumstances surrounding my daughter's death. Most of the time, I am thankful for gravity, but in this instance, it became my enemy. Still, it helps make her death comprehensible to me. I would not expect God to suspend gravity for my sake, or hers.

Faith can be integral in establishing a sense of the manageability of a loss, and a sense of meaningfulness following it. Even when we cannot believe in our own ability to cope, we may find strength in the assurance that "all things are possible for God" (Matt 19:26), or that we endure all these things through the power of [Christ] who gives [us] strength" (Phil 4:13). As followers of Christ, we believe in the power of God to redeem death and to transform suffering. This foundation can help us not only to find meaning in the midst of our darkest days but to become participants in the creation of it.

Finally, I encourage you to try two ancient practices that have helped deepen the faith of Christ followers for ages. Contemplation is the practice of sitting in the present moment with an awareness of God. You may think of contemplation as a prayer practice or as a meditation practice, and either one would be correct. As a prayer practice, contemplation may mean focusing your attention on an attribute of God, like

God's loving-kindness, peace, or sovereignty. Or, it might mean repeating a breath prayer. A breath prayer is a prayer that is meant to be repeated in rhythm with the breath. You can make a simple breath prayer by choosing a name for God that you will repeat as you inhale, and a one- or two-word request of God that you will repeat as you exhale. An example is the simple prayer, "Christ," (inhale) "have mercy," (exhale).

As a meditation practice, contemplation might simply be the act of noticing things in and around you. It can lead directly into the second practice that you may find healing and helpful, which is the practice of gratitude. By noticing simple things involving your five senses—the detail in a blade of grass, the smell of rain, the warmth of the sun on your face, the songs of the birds, the sweetness of an apple—you bring your awareness to the present moment and find something for which to be grateful. Both of these practices have been shown to help people cope, heal and improve their wellbeing.[5] Both can awaken an increased awareness of God and a deeper faith.

Chapter Five

GRIEF CAN BE COMPLICATED

Most of the time grief follows a natural healing process. As we discussed before, while it may not completely go away, it becomes less focal over time. However, some losses are harder to process and heal from than others. There are many factors that can complicate the grieving process. Complicated grief may not follow a normal healing process, and if your grief is prolonged or complicated, you may want to seek professional help. While professional counseling can be of benefit to almost anybody experiencing grief, certain circumstances call for more immediate attention than others.

When a death is unexpected and traumatic, for example, grieving can be more difficult. Suicide and homicide can be especially hard to grieve. But grief can also be more complicated when a death is prolonged and painful. If you had a difficult relationship with the person you lost—for example, if there was abuse, betrayal, conflict, or you just plain never really got along—your grief may be more problematic. And if you are grieving a loss that is not easily recognized by our society and/or not likely to be acknowledged by people around you from whom you need support, this can complicate your grief process as well; examples include, among others, miscarriage, abortion, the loss of your partner when your family or theirs did not accept your relationship, or the loss of a loved one who was incarcerated.

While the term "complicated grief" or "complicated bereavement" is what many mental health professionals have used for years to describe grief that may be clinical in nature, more recently grief researchers and theorists have begun to refer to "prolonged grief."[2] There is some debate in the field over whether "complicated grief" and "prolonged grief" are the same or distinct phenomena, and/or which is a better descriptor. I do not think it is necessary to get into the specifics of that here but wanted to introduce the language. What is more important for us to note is how to identify problematic grief and when to seek help.

In general, when it comes to deciding whether to seek treatment for any mental health issue, the best question to ask is, "How am I functioning?" If you are experiencing symptoms that interfere with your ability to function successfully at work, in school, or in your relationships or symptoms that are impairing your physical health, then whether or not your loss was complicated by any of the factors mentioned above, please seek out additional help. Talk to your doctor or a mental health provider. You do not have to suffer alone. If you are in danger of losing your job, failing in school, or alienating the people who are important to you, do not delay. If you have stopped taking your prescription medicine for a chronic health issue or are abusing alcohol or other substances to cope, please reach out before grief is no longer the primary issue.

And if you have a pre-existing mental health diagnosis, such as depression, anxiety, bipolar illness, post-traumatic stress, a psychotic disorder, or a substance use disorder, know that the stressor of grief places you at risk for an exacerbation of that illness or of relapse. Talk to your doctor or mental health provider. Ask those close to you to alert you if they think you start to exhibit additional signs or symptoms. Be especially sensitive to changes in your sleep and eating habits, with the awareness that these can signal a setback.

Finally, while thoughts of death or a wish to join your loved one are not uncommon during grief, thoughts of actively taking your own life should not be ignored. Talk to someone you trust who can help you seek additional help if needed—a friend, your doctor, your pastor, a mental health professional, or your local hospital emergency department. Crisis services are available in your area and can usually easily be found online or with a phone call to your local community mental health agency or emergency services. Life is worth living, and while you may not be able to believe it right now, your pain will not always be so great or so intense. It will get better, I promise.

I will end this little essay where I began, by reminding you that grief is a part of life for everyone. No one remains untouched by it. If you live long enough on this earth, your heart will one day be broken. If you love with all your heart, you will one day grieve with all your heart. Grief is a testament to love. The deeper we love, the deeper we grieve. But paradoxically, the greater the grief, also the greater the capacity for hope and joy. Those who have suffered most are often the ones who exhibit the fullness of life most visibly, have the most sensitive and beautiful spirits, and live the meaningful lives we all long for.

In a world fraught with loss, grief, and suffering, the best we can hope for is to learn to hold fast to that which can never be lost—the God of love to whom our souls will fly. God's love calls to us always, but sometimes it is in our grief that we are most able to hear. And sometimes it is through our healing that we are most able to serve as the channels through which God's love may flow to others and into all the world. This is my highest prayer for you in your deepest grief.

May God bless you in your grieving, and in your healing.

WHO HEALS?

God heals the brokenhearted
and bandages their wounds.

—*Psalm 147:3*

As we begin the process of examining grief in the light of faith, find comfort and hope in the knowledge that God has already begun a work of healing in you. Healing is not a process which you control or one which you perform yourself. You participate in the process by being open, holding out hope, and engaging in positive coping strategies, but you do not heal yourself. Healing is the work of God. On those days in which you struggle the most or feel the worst, cling to the knowledge that God is bandaging your wounds, and that God's healing is a process that happens despite you and often without your awareness.

Our bodies, like our spirits, are not impervious to injury, but they are made to heal. If you cut your finger, you do not have to concentrate on that injury or do any work to heal it. You may, depending on the circumstance, tend to it with special care, or seek out additional help. The act of healing, though, is generally outside of your control.

Healing is not always a linear process, and it is rarely instantaneous. The extent of the wound and the circumstances of an injury determine the length and complexity of the recovery. Sometimes pain is a part of healing—a sign that lets us know, counterintuitively, that we are headed in the right direction. Sometimes pain is a sign that we need to treat ourselves with extra patience and care. As you trust in God's loving care of your broken heart, ask for guidance that you may treat yourself gently and seek out additional support when it is needed.

God of the brokenhearted, help me trust in the unseen healing work
of your loving hands and to know that you bind my wounds and
restore my spirit, even in my deepest grief. Amen.

JOB

*A man in the land of Uz was named Job. That man was honest, a
person of absolute integrity; he feared God and avoided evil.*

—Job 1:1

The book of Job is unique in the Hebrew bible. Long considered
a book of wisdom in the Jewish tradition, it presents a different
picture of the nature of suffering than much of the Old Testament.
Traditionally, the Hebrew people understood suffering as a consequence
of disobedience and, therefore, as a punishment from God. Job presents
a very different understanding. From the outset, the reader is told that
Job is blameless in God's sight. He did nothing to deserve the calamities
that befall him, yet his suffering is exponential.

It is a natural part of the grief process to ask the question, "Why?"
We are wired to look for cause and effect and to order our experience.
It's natural to try to understand our role in our own suffering. This can
easily lead to misplaced feelings of guilt and self-blame.

Job does not offer a satisfactory explanation for the "why" of suffering, but it does unequivocally teach that Job did nothing to deserve
his great anguish. It was not his fault that his children perished or that
he lost his home, his possessions, and his health. Although the reader
is privy to this look behind the scenes, Job is not. He is left to struggle
with the same questions grieving people have struggled with throughout
the ages. The book of Job is a window into the process of grief, and you
may find comfort in the shared expression of your experience within its
pages.

*Lord, as I struggle to make sense of the "why" of this hurt and loss,
remind me that there are no easy answers. Assure me, instead, of
your love for me and for the one I grieve. Amen.*

COMPANIONS IN GRIEF

For sighing has become my daily food;
my groans pour out like water.
What I feared has come upon me;
what I dreaded has happened to me.
I have no peace, no quietness;
I have no rest, but only turmoil.

—Job 3:24-26 (NRSV)

Sighs, groans, fear, dread, restlessness, and turmoil—all of these experiences are familiar to anyone who has carried great emotional pain. Job begins this chapter with a wish that he had never been born. He curses the day of his birth (3:1-10). Barring that, he wishes that he had died at birth, or that he could choose to die rather than live in his current state of anguish. (v. 11-19) He expresses a sense of helplessness, powerlessness, and a lack of control. He cannot see a way out of his suffering. He feels trapped in it, and he blames God (v. 23).

Some scholars believe that passages from the book of Job are among the oldest writings in the Old Testament. In Job, we find one of the most poetic expressions of human suffering ever written. The words are ancient, but they continue to speak poignantly to the phenomenon of grief. There is something uniquely powerful about seeing your own experience captured perfectly in the words of another. As you find words that articulate completely an element of your grief in scripture (or other readings), write them down. Think of the person who wrote them, maybe a person in a completely different land at a completely different time, but one who shared your grief. Think of the wisdom of our God who created you both and give thanks

God, at times I feel trapped in this deep grief. I confess that I
question your place in it. I am not at ease. I sigh and groan. I am
afraid. Thank you for the voice of one who knows my anguish. In
his words, may I find your grace. Amen.

UNIMAGINABLE HOPE

What is my strength, that I should hope;
my end, that my life should drag on?

—Job 6:11

Job expresses utter despair. He compares the weight of his anguish to the sand of the seas (6:3). Under the heaviness of it, he relinquishes his hope for a future without grief. He believes he will have to carry it always, and that he does not have the strength to do so.

Grief is often described as a heaviness, a weight. Some people refer to this as a physical pressure, like a weight on their chests. Some explain it as a difficulty moving, like walking through water or mud. Even the air around them feels heavy. And some people express it as a heaviness of spirit; they carry a heavy heart.

Grief drains our strength and energy and steals our hope for the future, even if momentarily. It is hard to imagine or accept a future devoid of the one we miss desperately. Why should we be patient for future if we can't imagine that it will be any better?

Sometimes, in grief, we need to hope for a lighter and brighter future. Sometimes, we cannot. In these times, we need, instead, simply to carry the burden of grief through the next moment, hour, day. Moments become hours, hours become days, and days become months, and somehow, by the grace of God, we heal. The future comes, no matter our lack of hope in it, and we look back to see that what we once believed impossible has become a reality.

God, in my moments of despair, when I feel I cannot bear the weight of my anguish any longer, I cry out to you. When I cannot find hope for a future I did not want, I entrust it to you. Teach me the faith that comes from living moment by moment, clinging to your grace. Amen.

INEFFECTIVE HEALERS

You, however, are plasterers of lies;
ineffective healers, all of you.
Would that you were completely quiet;
that would be your wisdom.

—Job 13:4-5

Perhaps one thing the book of Job shows us is that people were no more effective at comforting the grieving long ago than we are now. Job calls his friends "ineffective healers." Job understands that he needs healing, and his friends are not helping. They try to offer words of wisdom, but the great insight of this passage is that the best wisdom they could possibly offer is not to be found in words, but in silence.

If you have been hurt by the words people have tried to offer you in grief, I am sorry. Know that this is an almost universal experience. Sometimes it is the words themselves that are inadequate or hurtful; sometimes it is the timing of those words. Either way, such words are not only ineffective but isolating. They add to our pain.

One of the best things anyone ever said to me when I was grieving was, "I don't know what to say, but I can sit and cry with you. I'm really good at that." Better yet is the simple act of sitting in silence with the tears of another.

Sometimes the people closest to us are waiting for us to ask for what we need. Often, it is a relief to know how we can help those we care about. If your closest friends or family are not offering you their silent company without being asked, consider telling them what you need. You might say, "I don't need you to say anything, but would you just come and sit with me?" Or, "It's okay if you don't know what to say. Don't say anything, just be with me. That's what I need."

Lord, I am surrounded by ineffective healers. When I feel alone,
remind me that my healing comes from you. Teach me to ask for
what I need, from you and my friends. Amen.

SEEING AND KNOWING

My ears had heard about you,
but now my eyes have seen you.

—*Job 42:5*

Finally, after many exchanges between Job and his friends, we hear from God. God does not answer Job's questions about his suffering, but God reminds Job of who God is—the omniscient, omnipotent Creator of all. God's self-revelation effectively silences Job. And interestingly, although Job has just heard from God, he affirms that he has seen God.

Often, I think we read the final chapters of Job with a focus on how God restored Job's life. But the most significant outcome of the book of Job is how God transformed Job's relationship with God. Job compares the difference in his understanding of God to the difference in having heard about a thing versus seeing it with his own eyes.

You have undoubtedly had the experience of meeting someone for the first time after having heard all about them. No matter how many times that person was described to you or how detailed the description, no description can capture the essence of a person; no description can adequately prepare us for meeting someone face-to-face. We know them almost instantly in a different way.

Job met God face-to-face in his suffering. And like Job, you have the opportunity to see God with your own eyes in yours. Your relationship with God can also be transformed by your grief, just as your grief can be transformed by your relationship with God.

Lord, reveal yourself to me, even in the depths of my grief. Amen.

COMPASSION

*When he saw her, the Lord had compassion for her
and said, "Don't cry."*

—Luke 7:13

In the book of Luke, there is a beautiful portrayal of the compassion of Jesus for the poor and grief-stricken. On his way to the town of Nain, he encounters a widow at the city gate whose only son is being carried out for burial. Jesus is deeply touched by her pain, and his compassion is such that he cannot simply pass by. Instead, he reaches out to her. "Do not weep," he says. Instinctively, he heals her son.

The mercy of Christ is such that he cannot help but enter into another's pain and offer comfort. So often, it is our human tendency to avoid the pain of another because of the feelings it evokes in us—helplessness, fear, insecurity, and the re-experiencing of our own grief. In all likelihood, you have observed such discomfort in those who avoid the subject of your loss and grief.

For this reason, grief can be very lonely. When you feel alone, recognize others' avoidance or unhelpful, distancing words as a window into their own struggles with grief. Look instead to those who, though they may not always find the right words, respond with empathy. Often, you will see your pain in their eyes. Accept their concern for you as a gift from God and their compassion as the heart of Christ. Remember the tender mercy of Jesus, who cannot help but enter into your pain, who speaks to you, as to this widow, with a gentle plea: "Do not weep." Receive his words not as a command not to cry, but as the expression they are, of his sincere longing to offer you comfort and healing.

Lord Jesus, I know that you understand my tears. You weep with me. You grieve with me. Offer me the desperately needed touch of your tender compassion this day. May I not turn away but embrace it. Amen.

THE WORK OF WAITING

I waited patiently for the LORD;
he turned to me and heard my cry.

—Psalm 40:1 (NIV)

Waiting patiently has never been my strong suit. In a culture that emphasizes action and accomplishment over inactivity and rest, patience and waiting are easily devalued. Yet grief often feels like a period of waiting. Learning to wait patiently, with both acceptance of the present and hope for the future, is a challenging task for the griever.

In my deepest grief, I read Psalm 40 daily. It served as a reminder to me that my "job" at that time was to wait patiently for God. It also reminded me that God was not oblivious to my suffering. God heard my cries. This psalm of thanksgiving is a story of God's salvation and redemption, told by one who was lifted out of deep despair and now testifies to the love and faithfulness of the One who saved him. My waiting, like the psalmist's, would not be in vain, and I clung to that hope. In the words of Psalm 40, I found the strength to keep waiting.

On some days, you may feel acutely that you are waiting. It may seem that there is nothing else to do and nowhere to find comfort. Such an awareness lends itself to frustration at best and at worst, despair. On those days, remember that rest and activity are two sides of the same coin. Both are necessary for healing. There is always a tension between them, a need for balance. Accept the moments of waiting with the knowledge that the time for activity will come. Know that God inclines God's ear to you and hears your cries. Find hope in the psalmist's testimony. One day, it will be your own.

Oh Lord, waiting is often the hardest work of all. In my darkest
moments and deepest despair, draw near to me. Incline your ear.
Hear my cry. Heal my broken heart. Amen.

STUCK IN THE MUD

He lifted me out of the slimy pit,
  out of the mud and mire;
he set my feet on a rock
  and gave me a firm place to stand.

—Psalm 40:2 (NIV)

Once, when I was about nine or ten years old, I was climbing on some rocks surrounded by mud on my family's farm. The ground was obviously soft, but I could not tell how deep the mud was until I stepped in, attempting to maneuver between rocks. I sank immediately and found myself stuck in mud up to my shins. I could not move. Every time I tried to take a step, I seemed to sink deeper. The mud and mire sucked at my feet, pulling me down. I was trapped, and I was afraid.

I don't think I could have freed myself from the mire without help. My dad, who was nearby, heard me calling out. He came and stood on the rock beside me, took me by the arms, and lifted me up. I came out of my shoes, but he pulled me to safety. I think of that experience when I read these words from Psalm 40.

Sometimes in the weeks and months following a loss, we know we are trapped in the miry depths of grief. Other times, confident that we are ready to move, we take a step forward. The ground seems to fall away, and we sink. The psalmist knows that no matter how long we spend in the pit, or how often we revisit it, God comes to lift us out. It may take time, but we have the assurance that we will be set on firm ground once again.

God of the pit and of the rock, remind me of your presence in my suffering. When I feel as if I am sinking, lift me. Set me on your rock when I need a firm place to stand. Amen.

KEEP LIVING

"But he is dead now. Why should I fast? Can I bring him back again? No. I am going where he is, but he won't come back to me."
— *2 Samuel 12:23*

Regardless of the circumstances of the conception, birth, and death of King David's first child with Bathsheba, and no matter that his response to the child's death probably betrays something of his flawed character and behavior, these words speak a fundamental truth about loss and grief: *It is best to go on living.*

We rely on the assurance that we will one day go to be with the ones we dearly love, but no amount of fasting, wailing, or pleading will bring about the thing we want most—for them to return to us. These words attributed to David capture the predicament precisely.

Some days, to go on living simply means going through the motions: getting out of bed and putting one foot in front of the other all day long. Other days, and over time, to go on living means to risk the potential of more hurt and grief by engaging fully in life and relationships, through love, joy, and laughter. Ultimately, each of us faces a choice: whether to wear grief like a suit of armor in an attempt to protect ourselves from the unpredictability of the world or to live and love freely in spite of the vulnerability it brings.

In my grief, I have often thought about my role in the continuing legacy of those I have loved and lost. In the end, I want to believe that their lives made me better and not that their deaths ruined me. I ask, how can I best honor the gift of their lives? How can I best honor the God who gave them?

Lord, thank you for the life of my loved one. In time, by your love and mercy, show me how to live in a way that honors their life.
Amen.

COMFORT

Comfort, comfort my people,
says your God.

—Isaiah 40:1

To the Jews who have been living in exile in Babylon with hopes of one day returning to their homeland, a simple but profound understanding of the nature and character of God is expressed. God comforts God's people.

God does not always protect God's people from harm, individually or collectively. Through destruction, conquest, and exile, the people of the Old Testament knew grief and despair. God's covenant people had every reason to feel abandoned by God and to fear that the covenant was void. Yet the prophets declare that God has not abandoned God's people. The covenant is intact. God hears their cries. God speaks tenderly. God comforts. And God will restore.

Comfort is a powerful relationship builder. As a parent, my greatest desire, always, is to protect my children from harm or distress. But I wonder, what would my relationship with them be if I had never had the opportunity or the need to comfort them? The closeness that was nurtured and the trust that was built upon many moments of comfort have been vital to the bond we now share.

The same can be said of my relationship with God. The solace and comfort I have found in God's word and God's presence during times of sorrow and heartache have been vital to the bond we share and to the deepening of my faith. Although I will never accept a theology which suggests that God orchestrated my, or especially my loved ones', suffering for the purpose of deepening our relationship, I can recognize the closeness God offers and give thanks for it, nonetheless.

God of comfort, I need you. Draw me near to your heart; your
solace is like none other. May your presence soften my woundedness.
If there is any hope for the healing of my soul, it is to be found in
you. Amen.

HELD BY CREATION

I raise my eyes toward the mountains.
    Where will my help come from?
My help comes from the LORD,
    the maker of heaven and earth.

—*Psalm 121:1-2*

Around my East Tennessee home, the mountains rise and ripple like the folds of a quilt, wrapping our little part of the world in beauty, majesty, and comfort. I love to look at them. In the winter, they are clothed in sleepy shades of purple and brown, etched in white. Clouds envelop them in a haze of listlessness. But come springtime, they will announce new life in myriad hues of green against a bright blue sky. Seasons will pass, and they will don their winter colors once again.

Hiking in the mountains speaks stillness to my soul. When I observe the changing seasons and consider how many springs and winters these mountains have witnessed, I cannot help but be aware of how small I am and how fleeting my days are. But I do not despair. Instead, I find peace in the knowledge of the vastness of creation and Creator. Such awareness awakens in me a sense of connectedness to God and to all things.

Psalm 121 may have been a pilgrimage song for those traveling to Jerusalem. The exact center of the poem is found in verse 5: "The LORD is your keeper." Awe at God's creation often inspires a sense of being held, kept, calmed, and comforted. Just as the mountains regularly evoke such awe for me, other parts of God's creation may do the same for you. The ocean, the stars, a sunset, a bird, a rock, the tiniest flower—may you find that same sense of being held and kept by God in any—or all—of these.

Maker of heaven and earth, I raise my eyes to look upon your creation. Remind me that my help comes from you. Amen.

IF ONLY

*The king trembled. He went up to the room over the gate and cried.
As he went, he said, "Oh, my son Absalom! Oh, my son! My son
Absalom! If only I had died instead of you! Oh, Absalom, my son!
My son!"*

—2 Samuel 18:33

Trying to make sense out of the death of those we love is an impossible task, but one which our minds cannot help but undertake. As we struggle to comprehend the reality of our loss, two questions often plague us. One we have already considered: "Why?" The other is, "What if…?"

It is normal to struggle with the "what ifs" of loss. "What if I had…?" "What if he/she had…?" Or sometimes these take the related form, "If only…" There are hundreds or even thousands of "What ifs" and "if onlys." Our minds seem primed to generate an endless supply. But for most of us, a few are predominate. We become convinced that "if only" we had done this or that, or our loved one had done this or that, or this or that had or had not happened, everything would be different. Sometimes "if onlys" take the form of things we wish we had said or done differently while we still had the chance or regrets about our final moments with the ones we love.

It is a natural defense of our psyches to try to undo our greatest pain. We search for some way to make the ending come out another way. The thing to know now is that regret is part of grief. If that "if only" you imagine had happened, you would likely be struggling with a different "if only" now.

David's words in this verse capture the underlying essence of all our "if onlys": "If only you were still alive."

Lord, if only the one I love were still here. I miss them so. Amen.

PRAYERS ON OUR BEHALF

In the same way, the Spirit comes to help our weakness. We don't know what we should pray, but the Spirit himself pleads our case with unexpressed groans.

—Romans 8:26

Questioning God, doubting God, and feeling anger toward God are normal parts of the grief experience for people of faith. Scripture suggests that this has always been the case. The writers of the psalms, for example, express hurt, disappointment, and feelings of rejection and anger. They ask tough questions of God. Such honest expressions provide a model for the appropriate and spiritually healthy way to manage our conflicted feelings about God during grief. We have the freedom to ask our questions and articulate our feelings. We do not have to be afraid to wrestle with God.

There are times, however, when we may not be able to do even this. It may be hard, or impossible, to pray at all. Here is a true, repeated prayer from my past: "Lord, I love you, but I cannot talk to you right now." I do not doubt that God received and blessed this prayer, in all its barrenness, to produce spiritual fruit in my life.

In my faith tradition, we sometimes use the language "Creator, Redeemer, Sustainer" as an alternative way of speaking about the Trinity. In the verse above from Romans, Paul is acknowledging the sustaining nature of the Holy Spirit during the times of our greatest weakness or spiritual emptiness. The image of God's Spirit praying when we cannot, interceding with groans too deep for words, is powerful. It has indeed sustained me through many dark nights and impossible days. If you find yourself unable to pray, take heart. God's love is so great that the Holy Spirit prays on your behalf always, with a depth of understanding way beyond your own.

Today, rest in the image of the Holy Spirit pleading your case with groans that words cannot express.

LOVE NEVER DIES

Love never fails.

—1 Corinthians 13:8

Love is our highest calling, our deepest desire, and the greatest mystery of the human experience. We are hard pressed to define or even describe it. Love gives our lives beauty and meaning. In fact, love gives us life. Life is born of love, and in the absence of the attachment bonds which sustain life, we cannot survive. We perish without love.

The absence of love causes death, but death does not cause the absence of love. This is the message of 1 Corinthians 13:8. Death cannot stop love. Love never dies. Love is eternal. Love always remains.

Stop for a moment and consider that your love for the one you grieve is eternal. Though he or she was taken from you, love can never be taken from you. And it has not been taken from your beloved. It can never be taken from either of you. Your love lives on.

Grief is often a searching, a yearning. We are hardwired to seek out, to search for, the objects of our love. We long for their physical presence, and when we cannot find them, we feel restless, anxious, and depressed. This is because of our continuing love for them, not the absence of it. With time, our physical selves—our brains and bodies—adapt to their physical absence. Our searching behavior stops or becomes infrequent, but this does not mean that our love ends. Often, it means that we have learned to experience the closeness of our loved ones without their physical presence, though most of us will still long for them from time to time.

In the midst of your longing and searching, hold fast to the knowledge that love never dies.

God of love, I ache to touch, to hold the one I've lost. I long to look into their eyes, to hold their hand, to breathe their scent, to hear their voice. Comfort me with love. Amen.

DETACHMENT

Though the fig tree doesn't bloom,
and there's no produce on the vine;
though the olive crop withers,
and the fields don't provide food;
though the sheep are cut off from the pen,
and there are no cattle in the stalls;
I will rejoice in the LORD.
I will rejoice in the God of my deliverance.

—Habakkuk 3:17-18

Praising God in the midst of suffering seems out of place. It is against our human nature. But it is completely consistent with our spiritual nature, and it has the power to lift us out of ourselves and into the presence of God. Even while remaining acutely aware of our suffering, we can sense God's vastness and presence. Spiritually mature people demonstrate this sort of detachment from their immediate circumstances and emotions—even their greatest suffering. They seem to have cultivated a constant awareness of God's presence and love, and it cannot be entirely shaken by even the gravest loss. The great Christian mystics, for example, write poetically of this sort of wisdom. They have learned what it means to abide in God. But such wisdom is not easily gained. It is borne of suffering, and struggle, and often comes only after a long period of spiritual drought and emptiness.

Job responds to his cataclysmic losses with these words: "The LORD has given; the LORD has taken; bless the LORD's name" (Job 1:21). If you feel barren, empty, and dry in your grief, be assured that even your barrenness, offered before God, can bear spiritual fruit. You may not have the emotional reserves to praise God right now, but when you have even a little, even a window of gratitude, give it to God and see what God will do.

The LORD has given; the LORD has taken; bless the LORD's name.
Amen.

GOD IS GOD

"He makes the sun rise on both the evil and the good and sends rain on both the righteous and the unrighteous."

—Matthew 5:45

These words from Matthew remind me again (and I need to be reminded often) that God is God, and I am not. When I blame myself for the loss of my beloved or ask why they deserved to die, when I ask whether I deserved to lose them or feel that I am being punished in my grief, these words suggest that such questions are misguided. They remind me instead to rely on God's sovereignty and find reassurance in God's impartiality. God makes the sun shine on the righteous and unrighteous and sends rain to both. God does not discriminate. Birth, life, healing, health, illness, and death touch all of God's creation.

Would I want it to be any other way? If I could have a god of my making, one who always protects the righteous from suffering and always punishes the wicked, one who withholds the sun and the rain from the evil but not the good, would I really want such a god? There is no room for redemption in an economy like that. Would I give up extravagant grace in favor of predictability? Because we cannot have both.

When my heart hurts, it is tempting to wish that God would behave in the way I want, to protect the things I want protected, even to alter the laws of the physical universe in order to do so. I want God to act according to my needs and desires and to keep my heart from hurting again. It is only natural to feel this way. But God will never acquiesce or submit to my expectations, and my soul does not really want God to, anyway.

Lord of all, in my pain, I cannot help but question the way you have ordered the universe. Teach me to give thanks that you are God and I am not, to rely on your sovereignty, impartiality, and love. Amen.

QUESTIONS

My plans aren't your plans,
nor are your ways my ways, says the LORD.

—*Isaiah 55:8*

This is my husband's favorite scripture. It became especially meaningful to him in the midst of his own grief. In it he found consolation in the acceptance that God's thoughts are so much higher than his, he could not even begin to understand God's ways.

When we ask God, "Why?" or, "How could you let this happen?" and don't feel like we get a good answer, perhaps it's not only that there are no easy answers. Perhaps the questions themselves do not even make sense, so small is our understanding in comparison to God's. My second grader sometimes asks me questions that I do not know how to answer. My understanding of the world is so different from his that the questions seem absurd. Where do I start? Can I even try to explain to him the problem with his question? I certainly cannot reply with advanced concepts or even vocabulary beyond his level. His developing brain simply is not able to comprehend.

Sometimes I try to answer his underlying question instead or address the emotion behind the question. Where did this question come from? What is his concern? What does he need? Often, he needs to know that I listen, that I love him, that we are partners in his growth and learning, and that he can trust me.

Sometimes what he needs is the reassurance that it is okay for him not to know. He does not have to understand, because he can depend on me for that.

God, may I relinquish my questions to the faith that your thoughts
and ways are high above mine. When I cannot understand,
strengthen my trust in you. Amen.

PRECIOUS TEARS

You yourself have kept track of my misery.
Put my tears into your bottle—
aren't they on your scroll already?

—Psalm 56:8

How many tears have you cried in your grief? You probably do not know, but God does. The psalmist's faith rested on the belief that God keeps track of our misery. God numbers tears, even collects them in a bottle.

Why might you count the tears of another? Why would these be precious to you? I would collect my children's tears out of hope, driven by my love for them and the desire to one day see those tears be redeemed by becoming agents of healing and wholeness.

With all my heart I believe in the love of our God who does not dismiss our tears but counts them as precious. God wants and works to transform our suffering and offers us hope. It is not empty hope. Our tears are not in vain. God has both the power and the desire to redeem them.

The faith stories of our ancestors are stories of redemptive love. Over and over again, when it seems as if all has been lost, we read about God's faithfulness and transforming power. The cross, the cornerstone of our faith, demonstrates God's redemptive love most of all. The cross should have meant the end of God's love for humanity; instead, it marked the culmination of that love.

If God would transform the crucifixion of Christ into the salvation of the world, what might God do with your tears?

Lord, I have cried too many tears to count, but I trust that each one has been precious to you. Only by faith can I hope that my tears have not been in vain. I count on the redemptive power of your love to transform them into something good, something lovely, something I cannot now imagine. Hold my sadness close to your heart. Amen.

A SHOULDER TO CRY ON

He will wipe away every tear from their eyes. Death will be no more. There will be no mourning, crying, or pain anymore, for the former things have passed away.

—*Revelation 21:4*

Crying alone can be one of the loneliest experiences. Many of us do not want to cry in front of others, so we wait until we have privacy to let our tears flow freely. While the tears can be cleansing and we may feel better afterward, the fact remains that crying alone is a deeply desolate experience.

One of the most intimate and comforting experiences is crying on the shoulder of another. When I think of times I have felt closest to my husband, I remember crying as he held me. When I think of times I have felt closest to my children, I taste the tears I have kissed from their cheeks. One of the most tender acts we offer to one another is the wiping away of tears. Most of us have given and received such tenderness, which is why this image of God wiping away every tear from the eyes of God's children is so poignant.

One of the most hopeful metaphors in the Bible is that of the New Jerusalem, a new heaven and a new earth. Our souls long for a better world: a new creation, one without death, mourning, crying, or pain. Our greatest hope is for an end to grief. Short of the realization of that hope, we cling to faith that God wishes it for us as well.

For now, we grieve. But we also hope. Today, may you find hope in the One who would wipe away every tear.

God, I find hope in the promise of a new creation, an end to death and suffering, a time without heartache. Until then, with a gentle hand, wipe away my tears. Amen.

A PRESENT HOPE

*But not only that! We even take pride in our problems, because
we know that trouble produces endurance, endurance produces
character, and character produces hope. This hope doesn't put us to
shame, because the love of God has been poured out in our hearts
through the Holy Spirit, who has been given to us.*

—Romans 5:3-5

Hope can be elusive to the suffering. Grasping at hope often awakens
the fear of being made a fool, and no one wants to be a fool. No
one wants to feel ashamed for hoping for the impossible.

There is one kind of hope that never disappoints. It is not a hope
that predicts what God will do but one that rests in the certainty of who
God is. We never know what God will do in the future. Usually, we
know it least when we think we know it most.

When our hope is based on the goodness of God rather than on
expectations for the future, it becomes realized in the present. God, in
God's infinite mercy and love, enters our present moment and works
within us with the power of healing that is always available to God.
When we read this scripture from Romans remembering to keep our
hope in God's character, suffering becomes a pathway to hope because
suffering draws us to God in a way that few things can.

*Lord, my hope is found in you alone. I cannot help but reach for
a future in which this pain I feel now is not so acute, in which my
heart is not so tender and raw. But help me to see the hope that
never disappoints, the hope that is available to me now, because of
who you are. Amen.*

REAL VS. TRUE

Where could I go to get away from your spirit?
Where could I go to escape your presence?
If I went up to heaven, you would be there.
If I went down to the grave, you would be there too!
If I could fly on the wings of dawn, stopping to rest only on the far side
of the ocean—even there your hand would hold me; even there your
strong hand would hold me tight!
                                                —Psalm 139:7-10

God is love. It is impossible to escape the presence of God, and if it is impossible to escape the presence of God, it is also impossible to escape the love of God.

Perhaps there are days in which you feel abandoned by God. If this is the case, do not be surprised. You are in good company. Even Jesus felt abandoned by God. Even Jesus asked for things from God which he did not receive. Remember how he poured out his heart to God, so desperate and fervent in his prayers that his sweat dripped with blood (Luke 22:44)? But God did not fulfill his request. Remember his anguished cry from the cross, asking why he had been forsaken (Matt 27:46; Mark 15:34)? Even Jesus felt alone.

One of the tasks for anyone in emotional distress is to learn to separate what we feel from what we know. Feeling abandoned, feeling alone, feeling like God does not care about your suffering does not make any of that so. The feelings are real, but they aren't true.

My children regularly accuse me of not understanding how they feel, or worse, not caring enough to give them what they want. Truthfully, in those times it takes every bit of restraint that I have not to give into their desires. I resist, because I see a bigger picture. I know things that they do not. I understand much more than they do about what they need in order to grow and mature. I resist because I believe it is what they need, and I intend to walk with them not only on this leg of the journey, but every step of the way.

◇◇

Lord, sometimes it seems that you are so far away. Help me to trust
that your strong hand holds me tight, even when I cannot feel it.
Amen.

◇◇

A SECRET WORTH KNOWING

"Peace I leave with you. My peace I give you. I give to you not as the world gives. Don't be troubled or afraid."

—*John 14:27*

The world gives trouble; Jesus gives peace. Steep yourself in that awareness for a good, long minute. The brokenness of the world has touched your heart and drained your spirit. Jesus offers you his peace, which transcends understanding.

It is impossible to describe the peace that passes understanding to someone who has not experienced it. But such peace seems to be more easily accessible, ironically, when we suffer and grieve. We often witness it at the moment of death. Perhaps that is because there is no other time when heaven and earth are so deeply connected or body and spirit so distinctly separate. I can remember walking outside one day after my daughter died and marveling at the sky. I was certain it had never been that particular shade of blue before. I was in awe, and I felt an awareness of God and a stillness, a peace, that was indescribable.

I have come to think of such sensitivity to the peace of God as the gift I did not want. I have felt as if I have been shown a great secret. I did not want to know it. I never would have chosen to know it, but I cannot deny that it is a secret worth knowing, and perhaps the most important thing I have ever learned. If given the choice, I might un-know it. But I know life is better having learned it.

In your grief, there are ways in which you are sensitive to the places where heaven touches earth, ways in which your spiritual awareness is heightened as at almost no other time. Do not miss that experience.

Lord Jesus, give me your peace. Amen.

FAITH IS HOPE

*I believe that the present suffering is nothing compared to the
coming glory that is going to be revealed to us.*

—Romans 8:18

With these words, Paul expresses the greatest Christian hope—that
whatever this world suffers is incomparable to the glory of God
that is being revealed. Perhaps your anguish is too deep right now
to see how it could possibly be matched or surpassed by anything beautiful, worthy, or glorious. Maybe your heartache is so deep that you
doubt you will ever witness glory or experience hope or joy again. Or
perhaps you are numb, and neither suffering nor hope are accessible to
you right now.

The Christian life is a life of faith. The writer of Hebrews reminds
us that faith is the reality of what we hope for, the proof of what we don't
see (Heb 11:1). Let that sink in for a moment. We tend to interpret this
verse as meaning that faith is believing that we will eventually see the
thing we hope for. But I wonder if that is what the writer had in mind.
I wonder if it is more accurate to say that our faith is the thing hoped
for. In other words, faith is of a higher value and more precious than
proof; it is worth more than the actual evidence of our greatest hope.
After all, as Paul goes on to say, "Who hopes for what he already has?"
(Rom 8:28).

Grief is like exercise for the muscles of faith. Nothing causes us to
long for a revelation of the glory of God like the heartache of loss. Paul
knew well and expressed articulately the suffering of a broken world, but
still found within the capacity for hope and faith.

*Lord, I need to know that there is something greater than my
suffering. Convince me that my heartache is not in vain. Amen.*

WEARIED ENOUGH TO SOAR

But those who hope in the LORD
will renew their strength;
they will fly up on wings like eagles;
they will run and not be tired;
they will walk and not be weary.

—Isaiah 40:31

Last year, I hiked with a friend to one of the most beautiful places I have ever seen. Thick green moss covered rocks and trees and every part of the landscape, like carpet. We had gone specifically to find the moss, having seen pictures of this lush, green, otherworldly paradise and wanting to experience it for ourselves. I felt as if I had entered the land of fairies.

But the climb was long and steep, and I doubted at times—especially during that last mile—that I would make it. It was one of the most strenuous hikes I have ever taken. When we finally made it to the top, I was completely exhausted. My body was weary and heavy. But my spirit was soaring. There was a fire tower at the top of the mountain. Because of my fear of heights, I could not climb all the way up, but at the top of the mountain my strength was renewed. I climbed high enough to see that the view was breathtaking. I climbed high enough to feel like I could fly.

My body was as weary as it had ever been that day, but the physical exhaustion was nothing in comparison to the weariness of my soul during grief. I would choose physical weariness over spiritual weariness any day. Still, sometimes experiencing one extreme heightens our ability to experience the opposite extreme. Spiritual weariness sometimes makes it possible for us to soar to new spiritual heights when our strength is renewed. Perhaps today you can only hope to walk and not be weary, but keep hoping in the Lord. You may soon find that you will "fly up on wings like eagles."

Lord, please renew my strength. My hope is in you. Amen.

NEVER FORGOTTEN

But Zion says, "The LORD has abandoned me;
my Lord has forgotten me."
Can a woman forget her nursing child,
fail to pity the child of her womb?
Even these may forget,
but I won't forget you.
Look, on my palms I've inscribed you;
your walls are before me continually.

—*Isaiah 49:14-16*

If you have ever felt forgotten by God, find reassurance in this metaphor. A new mother is more likely to forget the child she nurses than the Lord is to forget you. There is nothing more precious, tender, and intimate than the image of a mother nursing her newborn baby. And this is the image the prophet chooses to convey the power of God's love and remembrance. God does not forget God's children, not for a moment. Instead he etches them on his hands; they are part of him.

The image of God's children inscribed on the palms of his hands calls to mind for me the nail-scarred hands of Jesus Christ. According to John's gospel, the disciple Thomas refused to believe in the resurrected Christ until he saw those scars himself (John 20:24-28). When I put myself in the place of Thomas in that story, I wonder if Thomas refused to believe without seeing proof because he could not bear the pain of hope and disappointment again. Maybe the pain of hope and disappointment seems too much for you to bear, too.

If so, remember that Thomas's doubt did not negate the power of Christ's resurrection. Jesus had defeated the grave, whether Thomas was able to believe it or not. Neither is the power of God's love for you negated by your doubt or fear. God has inscribed you, and all God's children, on his palms. Your walls are ever before him.

Lord, when I wonder if you have forgotten me, remind me that you
have carved my name in your hand. Amen.

NO STRANGER TO SUFFERING

> *We don't have a high priest who can't sympathize with our
> weaknesses but instead one who was tempted in every way that
> we are, except without sin. Finally, let's draw near to the throne of
> favor with confidence so that we can receive mercy and find grace
> when we need help.*
>
> —*Hebrews 4:15-16*

Jesus can sympathize with our weakness. Because of this, we can be confident that when we come to him for help, he will meet our need with mercy and grace. There is great comfort to be found in the company of those who can sympathize.

In my grief I was blessed to be cared for by many people who had experienced wrenching losses and were willing to reach out through their own pain in order to help me carry mine. I found strength and encouragement in the knowledge that they were somehow surviving. They had found the courage and the will not only to go on but to thrive. Like an army of angels, they surrounded me and my family with understanding and love.

Even more restorative than the support of this army of fellow grievers, though, is the knowledge that through Christ's humanity and his suffering, he can sympathize with all of my pain and weakness. The God of the universe does not know my suffering in an abstract or distant way, but in a very real and intimate way. He chose not to keep himself removed from it but to enter into it fully and completely out of love for his creation. But Christ does not withhold himself from anyone. He chooses to experience the pain of us all.

*Lord Jesus, thank you for your compassion and for your mercy and
grace in my time of need. Amen.*

LEARNING TO TRUST

Trust in the LORD with all your heart;
*   don't rely on your own intelligence.*
Know him in all your paths,
*   and he will keep your ways straight.*

—Proverbs 3:5-6

These words from Proverbs are my favorite in all of the Bible. I could not have completed this devotional without including them, so powerful have they been in my journey of healing and growing in faith.

If I am honest, I want nothing more than to know, to understand, and to make sense of the world around me and my part in it. For my entire life, I have relied on my intelligence. I like to figure things out. I always have. I approach the world as if it were a puzzle. It is tempting to believe that if only I could find the right pieces and learn how they fit together, I could solve any problem.

But grief is not a problem to be solved, and the world cannot be controlled by my intelligence. When all of my knowledge and understanding failed me, I had no choice but to learn to trust. I could not have developed the kind of trust I have now as long as I could rely on myself and my own understanding. It was only when that crumbled in the midst of my grief that I learned to trust completely.

Belief may be an intellectual exercise, but trust is a heart matter.

As my trust has grown, God has not straightened the path before me so that I travel directly to the things I desire. Instead, I've learned that a straight path always leads to God. If I trust and seek to know God, I know I am headed in the right direction.

Lord, when I am tempted to rely on my intelligence, show me how to trust with all my heart. Amen.

BROKEN AND MADE NEW

So then, if anyone is in Christ, that person is part of the new creation. The old things have gone away, and look, new things have arrived!

—*2 Corinthians 5:17*

A couple of years ago, my family purchased a butterfly dome, and patiently watched five tiny, scrubby-looking painted lady caterpillars grow, cocoon, and emerge re-created from their chrysalides as elegant winged beings. It was an everyday miracle, happening right in our home, like a little taste of heaven, not lost on any of us.

The message of the butterfly is that the simple, plain, ordinary, and even ugly can be radically changed into the exquisite, splendid, and magnificent. I long to know this truth, to believe in the promise of redemption for all things. During the most painful season of my life, butterflies became especially meaningful to me. A powerful symbol of transformation and new life, the butterfly spoke to my deepest need in my darkest hour: *hope.*

It occurs to me that butterflies are some of the few species that actually experience two births and two remarkably different lives. I have read that when a caterpillar is changing inside a chrysalis, the process involves a complete breaking down of the original organism. In other words, if you open a chrysalis during the middle of the process, you would likely find a gob of goo, not bearing any resemblance to either the caterpillar or the butterfly. The caterpillar is not only transformed; it is completely broken down so that it can be re-formed. Sometimes brokenness makes new life possible.

God, when I feel completely broken down, remind me of the example of the butterfly and of your transforming grace. May I find my hope, always, in you, blessed Redeemer. Amen.

MAKE WAY FOR NEW LIFE

Look! I'm doing a new thing;
*   now it sprouts up; don't you recognize it?*
I'm making a way in the desert,
*   paths in the wilderness.*

—*Isaiah 43:19*

I want to conclude our time together with this reminder. Take heart. God is making a way in the desert of your grief, a path in the wilderness of your suffering.

Our Creator is always doing a new thing. It is in God's nature to create, to renew, and to redeem. God does not stop God's creative work. Though you are immersed in an ending, a loss, a death, all around you are beginnings, victories, and births. Even within you, God desires to do a new thing. God does not require you to relinquish the object of your love in order to do this new work. We do not have a finite amount of love to offer. God, the source of our love, is infinite. By the power of the Holy Spirit, we continue to love the ones we have lost to death, even as we learn to extend our love in new ways and into new relationships.

God's work of healing your heart will continue over your lifetime. As you find yourself able to love again and as you find yourself loving again, you may realize that renewed love is both the result and the source of your healing. So it is with the One who created us in God's image with the capacity to love and to grieve so deeply. They are so closely entwined that sometimes it is hard to tell the difference between the two.

May you awaken from the dark night of your grief to feel the warmth of the sun once more.

God, when I can think of nothing but the past, nothing but the former things, help me to see the new work your hands are bringing forth. I thank you for the new thing you are doing in me, in and through my grief, even when I cannot see it. Amen.

NOTES

2. GRIEF IS INDIVIDUALIZED

1. Elisabeth Kübler-Ross, *On Death and Dying: What the Dying Have to Teach Doctors, Nurses, Clergy, and Their Own Families* (New York: Simon & Schuster, 1969).

2. J. Bowlby and C. M. Parkes, "Separation and loss within the family," in E. James Anthony and Cyrille Koupernik, eds., *The Child in His Family,* Yearbook of the International Association of Child and Adolescent Psychiatry and Allied Professions (New York: Wiley, 1970), 197–216.

3. J. William Worden, *Grief Counseling and Grief Therapy, Fourth Edition: A Handbook for the Mental Health Practitioner* (New York: Springer, 2009).

4. Therese A. Rando, *Treatment of Complicated Mourning* (Champaign, IL: Research Press, 1993).

5. S. Schuchter and S. Zisook, "The course of normal grief," in Margaret Stroebe, Wolfgang Stroebe, and Robert O. Hansson, *Handbook of Bereavement: Theory, Research and Intervention* (Cambridge: Cambridge University Press, 1999), 23–43.

6. George A. Bonanno, *The Other Side of Sadness: What the New Science of Bereavement Tells Us about Life after Loss* (New York: Basic Book, 2010).

7. M. Stroebe and H. Schut, "The Dual Process Model of Coping with Bereavement: Rationale and Description," *Death Studies* 23.3 (1999): 197–224.

8. Robert A. Neimeyer, *Meaning Reconstruction and the Experience of Loss* (Washington, DC: American Psychological Association, 2001).

9. Neimeyer, *Meaning Reconstruction and the Experience of Loss.*

3. GRIEF TAKES TIME

1. C. S. Lewis, *A Grief Observed* (New York: Bantam, 1983).

4. GRIEF CANNOT BE CONTROLLED

1. W. T. Hoyt and D. G. Larson, "What Have We Learned from Research on Grief Counseling? A Response to Schut and Neimeyer," *Bereavement Care* 29 (2010): 10–13.

2. K. A. Balkie and K. Wilhelm, "Emotional and Physical Health Benefits of Expressive Writing," *Advances in Psychiatric Treatment* 11.5 (2005): 338–46.

3. George A. Bonanno, *The Other Side of Sadness: What the New Science of Bereavement Tells Us about Life after Loss* (New York: Basic Book, 2010).

4. Aaron Antonovsky, *Health, Stress and Coping,* The Jossey-Bass Social and Behavioral Science Series (San Francisco: Jossey-Bass, 1979).

5. R. A. Emmons and M. E. McCullough, "Counting Blessings Versus Burdens: An Experimental Investigation of Gratitude and Subjective Well-Being in Daily Life," *Journal of Personality and Social Psychology* 84.2 (2003): 377–89.

5. GRIEF CAN BE COMPLICATED

1. N. A. S. Farb, A. K. Anderson, H. Mayberg, J. Bean, D. McKeon, and Z. V. Segal, "Minding One's Emotions: Mindfulness Training Alters the Neural Expression of Sadness," *Emotion* 10.1 (2010): 25–33.

2. George A. Bonanno, *The Other Side of Sadness: What the New Science of Bereavement Tells Us about Life after Loss* (New York: Basic Book, 2010).

Made in United States
North Haven, CT
22 November 2022

27109947R00039